Theater Masters' Take Ten
Volume I

Donna's First Brazilian
Lydia Blaisdell

English Lesson
Paula Vesala

The Battle of Coney Island
David Jacobi

Nordic Ambition (Self Portrait #3)
Phillip Howze

Of Our Own
Matthew Capodicasa

Off Tackle Glide
Sean David DeMers

Laodamiad
Chas LiBretto

Time Difference
Lin Tu

A SAMUEL FRENCH ACTING EDITION

SAMUEL FRENCH
FOUNDED 1830

SAMUELFRENCH.COM
SAMUELFRENCH-LONDON.CO.UK

Introduction Copyright © 2015 by Julia Hansen
DONNA'S FIRST BRAZILIAN Copyright © 2015 by Lydia Blaisdell
ENGLISH LESSON Copyright © 2015 by Paula Vesala
THE BATTLE OF CONEY ISLAND Copyright © 2015 by David Jacobi
NORDIC AMBITION (SELF PORTRAIT #3)
Copyright © 2015 by Phillip Howze
OF OUR OWN Copyright © 2015 by Matthew Capodicasa
OFF TACKLE GLIDE Copyright © 2015 by Sean David DeMers
LAODAMIAD Copyright © 2015 by Chas LiBretto
TIME DIFFERENCE Copyright © 2015 by Lin Tu
All Rights Reserved

THEATER MASTERS' TAKE TEN VOLUME I (including *DONNA'S FIRST BRAZILIAN, ENGLISH LESSON, THE BATTLE OF CONEY ISLAND, NORDIC AMBITION (SELF PORTRAIT #3), OF OUR OWN, OFF TACKLE GLIDE, LAODAMIAD,* and *TIME DIFFERENCE*) is fully protected under the copyright laws of the United States of America, the British Commonwealth, including Canada, and all other countries of the Copyright Union. All rights, including professional and amateur stage productions, recitation, lecturing, public reading, motion picture, radio broadcasting, television and the rights of translation into foreign languages are strictly reserved.

ISBN 978-0-573-70463-5

www.SamuelFrench.com
www.SamuelFrench-London.co.uk

For Production Enquiries

United States and Canada
Info@SamuelFrench.com
1-866-598-8449

United Kingdom and Europe
Plays@SamuelFrench-London.co.uk
020-7255-4302

Each title is subject to availability from Samuel French, depending upon country of performance. Please be aware that *THEATER MASTERS' TAKE TEN VOLUME I* (including *DONNA'S FIRST BRAZILIAN, ENGLISH LESSON, THE BATTLE OF CONEY ISLAND, NORDIC AMBITION (SELF PORTRAIT #3), OF OUR OWN, OFF TACKLE GLIDE, LAODAMIAD,* and *TIME DIFFERENCE*) may not be licensed by Samuel French in your territory. Professional and amateur producers should contact the nearest Samuel French office or licensing partner to verify availability.

CAUTION: Professional and amateur producers are hereby warned that *THEATER MASTERS' TAKE TEN VOLUME I* (including *DONNA'S FIRST BRAZILIAN, ENGLISH LESSON, THE BATTLE OF CONEY ISLAND, NORDIC AMBITION (SELF PORTRAIT #3), OF OUR OWN, OFF TACKLE GLIDE, LAODAMIAD*, and *TIME DIFFERENCE*) is subject to a licensing fee. Publication of this play(s) does not imply availability for performance. Both amateurs and professionals considering a production are strongly advised to apply to Samuel French before starting rehearsals, advertising, or booking a theatre. A licensing fee must be paid whether the title(s) is presented for charity or gain and whether or not admission is charged. Professional/Stock licensing fees are quoted upon application to Samuel French.

No one shall make any changes in this title(s) for the purpose of production. No part of this book may be reproduced, stored in a retrieval system, or transmitted in any form, by any means, now known or yet to be invented, including mechanical, electronic, photocopying, recording, videotaping, or otherwise, without the prior written permission of the publisher. No one shall upload this title(s), or part of this title(s), to any social media websites.

For all enquiries regarding motion picture, television, and other media rights, please contact Samuel French.

MUSIC USE NOTE

Please visit SamuelFrench.com to download the sound file required for NORDIC AMBITION (SELF PORTRAIT #3).

Licensees are solely responsible for obtaining formal written permission from copyright owners to use copyrighted music in the performance of this play and are strongly cautioned to do so. If no such permission is obtained by the licensee, then the licensee must use only original music that the licensee owns and controls. Licensees are solely responsible and liable for all music clearances and shall indemnify the copyright owners of the play(s) and their licensing agent, Samuel French, against any costs, expenses, losses and liabilities arising from the use of music by licensees. Please contact the appropriate music licensing authority in your territory for the rights to any incidental music.

IMPORTANT BILLING AND CREDIT REQUIREMENTS

If you have obtained performance rights to this title, please refer to your licensing agreement for important billing and credit requirements.

THEATER MASTERS STAFF

Founder and Artistic Director: Julia Hansen
Associate Artistic Director/Managing Director: Naomi McDougall Jones
Artistic Advisor: Andrew Leynse
Literary Manager, Aspiring Playwrights Competition: Chip Winn Wells
Teaching Artist: Kristin Carlson

Advisory Board:
Chris Ashley, Alec Baldwin, André Bishop, Gordon Davidson, Scott Ellis, A.R. Gurney, Doug Hughes, Judy Kaye, Andrew Leynse, John Lithgow, Robert Moss, Brian Murray, Jack O'Brien, Neil Pepe, John Rando, Theresa Rebeck, Tim Sanford

Board of Directors:
Julia Hansen, Susan Buckley, Nancy Dunlap, Jerry Finger, Betty Gates, Marilyn Greene, John Hoffman, Gerri Karetsky, Marianne Lubar, Staman Ogilvie, Mike Otte, Virginia Pearce, Jessica Salet, Jan Sarpa, Kimberly Schlosser, Marie Seidl, Nancy Stevens, Hal Thau, Charlotte Tripplehorn

Take Ten 2015 Staff

2015 National Adjudicator: Kathleen Chalfant
Assistant Producer: Maria Aparo
Production Stage Manager: Mark C. Hoffner
Technical Director: Brett Maughan
Set Designer: R. Thomas Ward
Prop Designer: Makia Martin
Casting Directors: Scott Wojcik & Gayle Seay

Cast of Aspen, Colorado Production: Heather Ardley, Dan Bosko, Jimmy Coates, Gerald DeLisser, Shannon Dick, Ed Foran, Lyon Hamill, Rett Harper, Naomi Havlen, Whitney Hewitt, Web Heyliger, Sophia Kai Higbie, Amy Kaiser, China Kwan, Graham Northrup, Emery Major, Luis Martinez, Travis Lane McDiffett, Naomi McDougall Jones, Talitha McDougall Jones, Heather Miller, Brad Moore, Willie Moseley, Haver Muss-Nichols, Wendy Perkins, Eileen Seeley, Summer Thomas, Chip Winn Wells, Chris Wheatley, Ryan Young

INTRODUCTION

This first published anthology of Theater Masters' plays comes as we head into the tenth year of our National MFA Playwrights Festival.

I founded the National MFA Playwrights Festival and Competition in 2007 for the same reason I founded The Director's Project while president of The Drama League of New York – I saw a need for an organization to bridge the gap between the training theater artists receive and the professional careers that lay ahead of them.

The National MFA Playwrights Festival provides a sequential training process that begins in a regional theater environment and culminates in NYC. No other opportunity like this exists.

Each September, Theater Masters solicits submissions from a select number of Master of Fine Art programs: Brown, CalArts, Carnegie Mellon, Columbia, Fordham/Primary Stages, University of Iowa, Northwestern, NYU, UCLA, UCSD, University of Texas at Austin, and Yale. These schools have been selected because of the outstanding training they provide. Submissions are read and rated by a panel of theater artists and then, using these ratings, along with the input of myself, our Associate Artistic Director, Naomi McDougall Jones, and our Distinguished Adjudicator, up to ten plays are ultimately chosen. The plays in this anthology were adjudicated by the distinguished actress, Kathleen Chalfant. Past Distinguished Adjudicators have included Christopher Durang, John Guare, A.R. Gurney, William Luce, Terrence McNally, Theresa Rebeck, Alfred Uhry, Eric Bogosian, Gordon Davidson, John Lithgow, Robert LuPone, and the late Lanford Wilson.

The program begins in January, when the winning playwrights, along with a professional team of directors and designers, are brought to Aspen to present an evening of theater, *Take Ten*, performed by a talented group of local actors. The writers are able to see their work in front of a sophisticated, receptive, inquiring audience and are given a critique by our Artistic Advisor, Andrew Leynse of Primary Stages and the Distinguished Adjudicator.

In the ensuing two months, the playwrights have an opportunity to re-write their plays, based on their experience in Aspen, and then given further professional feedback.

With the scripts now ready, the playwrights are brought to New York and, with the same directors and production team, the new drafts of the plays are mounted with an Equity cast. These productions are attended by New York audiences, as well as by top industry professionals. This, along with Wonder Week, an intensive in which we provide meetings and panels with key industry members, provides these young writers the chance to meet and develop relationships with those professionals who will remain treasured contacts for the rest of their careers.

I am proud that the National MFA Playwrights Festival can already claim two Pulitzer finalists, a Fulbright winner, and writers who have gone on to have productions at Lincoln Center, Roundabout, Playwrights Horizons, Manhattan Theatre Club, Second Stage, The Kennedy Center, as well as at a number of other important regional theaters.

I will be forever grateful to all who have given support through financial and in-kind donations and to the Board of Directors and to our Artistic Advisory Committee for making this program possible and dreams come true for our playwrights.

I am pleased to now share with you the winning plays from our 2015 National MFA Playwrights Festival.

Sincerely,

Julia Hansen
Founder and Artistic Director

TABLE OF CONTENTS

DONNA'S FIRST BRAZILIAN 9
ENGLISH LESSON 23
THE BATTLE OF CONEY ISLAND......................37
NORDIC AMBITION (SELF PORTRAIT #3) 49
OF OUR OWN..59
OFF TACKLE GLIDE 75
LAODAMIAD..87
TIME DIFFERENCE 103

Donna's First Brazilian

Lydia Blaisdell

DONNA'S FIRST BRAZILIAN was first produced by Theater Masters (Julia Hansen, Artistic Director; Naomi McDougall Jones, Associate Artistic Director/Managing Director) in New York City on April 28, 2015. The performance was directed by Margot Bordelon. The cast was as follows:

DONNA	Catherine Curtin
RECEPTIONIST	Peregrine Heard
PHILIPPA	Anna Weng
JOSEFINA	Megan Hill

CHARACTERS

DONNA – In her late 40s or early 50s. Strong. An accomplished woman, but out-of-her-element in this setting.

RECEPTIONIST – Early 20s. Perky and fashionable.

PHILIPPA – Stunning and not overly kind. Late 20s, early 30s. Might have feathers on her shoes.

JOSEFINA – Preferably Brazilian or Dominican. 30s. No-nonsense. Good at her job.

TIME

The present.

PLACE

A very upscale waxing salon in a major metropolitan area.

Scene One

(The fancy reception area of a high-end waxing salon and a treatment room.)

(Almost everything is white. **DONNA** *enters, carrying a series of bags. Bloomingdale's. Sephora.)*

RECEPTIONIST. Do you have an appointment?

DONNA. No.

RECEPTIONIST. What service would you like today?

DONNA. I'd like *(She leans in.)* a Brazilian.

RECEPTIONIST. Okay. Let me see who's available.

DONNA. I'd like a woman.

RECEPTIONIST. All of our estheticians are women.

*(***DONNA*** is lingering near the desk.)*

You can just have a seat right there.

*(***DONNA*** sits.)*

PHILIPPA. Hi. I'm here for my 4:30.

RECEPTIONIST. I have you with Alessandra for a Vajazzle in twenty minutes.

PHILIPPA. If you could squeeze me in sooner, that'd be fab.

RECEPTIONIST. She's with a client, but she'll be out shortly.

PHILIPPA. Okay.

DONNA. Hi there. I'm Donna.

PHILIPPA. Hi.

DONNA. This is my first time.

PHILIPPA. Excuse me?

DONNA. I've never… *(She gestures.)* before you know?

PHILIPPA. Oh. That's uh. That's great.

DONNA. My ex-husband never cared. Or looked.

PHILIPPA. Uh huh.

DONNA. Once you've born a man's children he can't exactly complain about the state of your hoo-ha.

PHILIPPA. I wouldn't know.

DONNA. What's a vajizzle?

PHILIPPA. Va-Jah-zul. They add rhinestones. To make it prettier. Or like a little flag if you want to celebrate Memorial Day or whatever.

DONNA. Jesus.

PHILIPPA. I feel like a sexy mermaid after.

DONNA. You don't do it for a guy?

PHILIPPA. God no. I'm single.
 I like the ease. Less prickly.

DONNA. Does it hurt?

PHILIPPA. At first, yeah. Helps if you pop an aspirin.

(*She offers.* **DONNA** *accepts.*)

DONNA. I am here because I have a date. And I overheard my daughter telling her friends that a Brazilian was "clutch date prep." So I thought I would treat myself.

RECEPTIONIST. (*to* **DONNA**) Josefina's ready to take you now.

PHILIPPA. Good luck!

(**DONNA** *is lingering again.*)

 Just think ahead to all the really exceptional sex you'll have. Guys go mad for it.

DONNA. I don't know about that.

PHILIPPA. You'll look *stunning*. Like. His jaw will be floating in an ocean of drool.

DONNA. Thanks.

(**DONNA** *crosses out.*)

PHILIPPA. Did you see that business?

RECEPTIONIST. I thought she was sweet.

(**PHILIPPA** *grimaces.*)

(The appointment room.)

JOSEFINA. So here are some wipes in case you want to freshen up. I'll give you a minute to undress and then we'll get started okay sweetheart?

DONNA. *(fast and awkward)* This is my um. My first time.

JOSEFINA. Oh. Honey. Of course. I'll go slow.

DONNA. So I take off what exactly?

JOSEFINA. Okay what are we doing today?

DONNA. A Brazilian.

JOSEFINA. Everything below the belt.

DONNA. Oh. Okay.

Great.

(DONNA undresses. JOSEFINA stirs pots of wax or cleans instruments.)

JOSEFINA. Great. I'm going to start at the top okay?

(JOSEFINA arranges DONNA. She spreads wax.)

Now when I say breathe, I want you to take a nice long breath in and then when I tell you to breathe out, you're going to exhale. Ready? Breathe in.

(DONNA breathes.)

And out.

(She rips the first strip off.)

DONNA. RATS.

Doggone it that hurts.

JOSEFINA. I'm sorry.

DONNA. You should warn people.

JOSEFINA. Ready?

DONNA. I'm good. I can do this. I was in the first class of women to graduate from Columbia.

(JOSEFINA preps another strip.)

How often do women *do* this?

JOSEFINA. About every six weeks.

(**JOSEFINA** *rips another strip.*)

DONNA. Oh sweet Baby JESUS. I thought you were going to warn me?

JOSEFINA. Sometimes it helps to not think about it.
This a treat for your hubby?

DONNA. No.
We're not together anymore.

JOSEFINA. Sorry to hear that.

DONNA. Don't be.
He was an asshole.

JOSEFINA. Men can be very difficult.

DONNA. Yes, but there is *difficult* and then there is a man that dropped five hundred seventy-nine dollars on an authentic Boba Fett reproduction.

JOSEFINA.

DONNA. The bounty hunter. From *Star Wars*.

JOSEFINA. I'm not / much of a –

DONNA. It's fine.
I'm better off now regardless.

JOSEFINA. Great. Now breathe.

DONNA. I am breathing.
I am strong.

JOSEFINA. Right on, sister.

(*She rips.*)

So what *is* the occasion? New man? Just for you?

DONNA. Yep. Third date. We're going to a downtown dance show this weekend.

(**JOSEFINA** *rips.*)

I'm hoping to *seal* the *deal*.

JOSEFINA. Good to get back in the saddle.
Ride that stallion.

DONNA. At this point, I'd settle for a pony.

JOSEFINA. You nervous?

DONNA. A little. My last date was in 1987.

JOSEFINA. You don't forget.

In. And.

    *(**DONNA** braces. **JOSEFINA** rips.)*

DONNA. Oh. That wasn't too bad.

JOSEFINA. You are going to look so gorgeous when we're through honey. Just clean and fresh and ready. It's much easier than shaving.

DONNA. Shaving?

JOSEFINA. Wow.

And in. And out.

    *(She rips. This one is a doozy. **DONNA** flinches hard.)*

DONNA. WHAT THE HELL IS WRONG WITH YOU?

JOSEFINA. Breathe.

DONNA. Do you enjoy making innocents suffer?

JOSEFINA. I'm almost done with this side. Now put your other leg up like. That's. Here. Like this. Yeah. That's great. I'm going to do the back now.

DONNA. The back?

JOSEFINA. You said Brazilian.

DONNA. The back, like my butt?

JOSEFINA. Just a little bit.

    (She spreads the wax.)

DONNA. You're joking.

JOSEFINA. Should I stop?

DONNA. No. I got this. I yanked a flunking daughter through calculus. I bailed my son out of a prison after he threw that paint bucket at a cop.

JOSEFINA. You got this.

The first time is the worst.

In. And out.

    (She rips. This one is a motherfucker.)

(**DONNA** *convulses in pain and jerks upright.*)

That one might bruise a little. You flinched.

DONNA. I need a minute.

JOSEFINA. Want to take a look?

DONNA. Yeah. Yes. I would.

(**JOSEFINA** *hands* **DONNA** *a mirror.* **DONNA** *looks.*)

I look so...

JOSEFINA. The swelling and redness will be gone in a few hours. I'll give you cortisone cream.

DONNA. I look like a child.

JOSEFINA. Like a teenager.

DONNA. I miss them.

JOSEFINA. What?

(**DONNA** *strokes her missing pubes.*)

DONNA. I miss my pubic hair. I never really thought about it. But seeing it so barren –

JOSEFINA. It's just a change.

DONNA. I can't believe Cheryl does this to herself every time she has a date.

JOSEFINA. Cheryl?

DONNA. My daughter.
She's 19.

JOSEFINA. Shall we get started again?

DONNA. Look, Josefina, you seem like a lovely person, but I don't think this is working for me.

(**DONNA** *gets up and begins to dress.*)

JOSEFINA. We aren't finished.

DONNA. I can't.

JOSEFINA. I didn't get the left side or the back. I'll take it in smaller pieces.

DONNA. You are *hurting* me. And I will not endure that pain further. I was a town comptroller. I am on the board of ROAR. I have *children*.

JOSEFINA. You can't just walk out of here like a plucked chicken.

DONNA. Watch me.

Who cares that this dude is relatively fit? Who gives a shit that I like the way he wears his hair or that he can actually converse about the recent elections in Kenya?

I bet he's not down at the barbershop mowing *his lawn*.

JOSEFINA. Are you sure that you want to leave?

DONNA. Absolutely. If he doesn't want me, bush and all, I will wait for someone who wants a *woman*.

JOSEFINA. If you change your mind, come back tomorrow before three, I'll finish you up for free.

DONNA. And I am going to have a talk with Cheryl.

(*She drops a hundred in* **JOSEFINA***'s palm.*)

This should cover it.

RECEPTIONIST. Are you alright?

DONNA. I have to go.

(*She re-adjusts her pants [there's wax sticking to her.]*)

Thanks for the pep talk. But this isn't something I'm up for.

PHILIPPA. What?! Don't tell me you are walking out of here half-waxed?!?!

DONNA. I'm going to pour myself a glass of Malbec and try to forget that women pay people to do this *business* to their lady parts. You want to join me?

PHILIPPA. I / don't think I can.

DONNA. No grown man should want your hoo-ha to have rhinestones glued to it.

PHILIPPA. Aren't you worried? I mean how does it look?

DONNA. I have varicose veins and cellulite and an ass that's aiming for my shins. The state of my pubic hair is a minor concern.

PHILIPPA. Hurts less every time.

DONNA. Last chance. C'mon. I want to buy you a wine or a craft beer or whatever young people drink and find out how to get a little action.

PHILIPPA. I can't just cancel / my appointment.

DONNA. Do I just tell my date I'm ready to fuck?

PHILIPPA. I don't know if I would / just blurt it out.

RECEPTIONIST. Is everything okay ma'am?

DONNA. Freaking fantastic.

PHILIPPA. I shouldn't.

DONNA. *Please?*

These aren't questions I can ask my daughter.

PHILIPPA. *(to the* **RECEPTIONIST***)* I'm sorry, I'm going to cancel today's appointment.

DONNA. There's a great little wine bar around the corner.

PHILIPPA. Okay.

DONNA. Are diaphragms still the best / form of contraception?

PHILIPPA. God no.

*(***PHILIPPA** *and* **DONNA** *exit together.)*

*(***JOSEFINA** *comes out, a slump to her shoulders.)*

RECEPTIONIST. That lady is never coming back. Whackjob. I'm ordering Thai, you want something?

JOSEFINA. I'm good, thanks.

RECEPTIONIST. Aww, don't sulk. Wasn't your fault. Your technique is flawless.

JOSEFINA. She looked like my aunt. The one who gave me my first deep fried Oreo.

RECEPTIONIST. I'm getting you a summer roll.

JOSEFINA. Okay.

RECEPTIONIST. Date tonight?

JOSEFINA. Does my pocket rocket count?

RECEPTIONIST. Wasn't there that new girl? The one with the piercing and the hair?

JOSEFINA. Flew the coop.

RECEPTIONIST. We could go dancing? There's that club under the bridge I've been meaning to go to forever.

JOSEFINA. Not tonight.

RECEPTIONIST. Oh.

> *(They sit there for a moment. A shuffling of feet. A checking of phones.)*

> *(And then the **RECEPTIONIST**'s phone rings:)*

(into the phone) Good afternoon. What service would you like today? Oh. Oh yes. We do custom shapes all the time. What would you like? Well my esthetician is right here, I can check with her. One minute.

> *(**JOSEFINA** looks up.)*

Can we do a *lightning bolt?*

> *(**JOSEFINA** nods.)*

Yes, I've just checked with our specialist. We can manage that. Oh no, thank *you.* Yes, I *know.* When would you like to come in?

> *(blackout)*

End of Play

English Lesson

Paula Vesala

ENGLISH LESSON was first produced by Theater Masters (Julia Hansen, Artistic Director; Naomi McDougall Jones, Associate Artistic Director/Managing Director) in New York City on April 28, 2015. The performance was directed by Joseph Ward. The cast was as follows:

NENA..Andrea Gallo
TOMMI .... Andre Gulick and Sophie Wright
LAURA.. Heli Serviö

CHARACTERS

NENA – An old Puerto Rican woman with Alzheimer's disease. Her appearance is somehow fragile, and her walking is slow, shaky and difficult. Her voice is not strong. She is wearing a long worn-out t-shirt and health sandals. Added to the worn-out look she could have something glamorous or colorful, like a necklace that doesn't fit the t-shirt at all. She speaks with an accent.

TOMMI (*Tohmee*) – A ten-year-old Finnish boy. Normal boy's clothes, muted colors (gray, blue etc.). Shy, observant.

LAURA – Tommi's mother. Finnish. Laura is about 35 years old. Down-to-earth clothes with muted colors, like a gray shirt and jeans or capris. Has an accent.

MR. DORROS – (One of the neighbors) can be heard practicing the piano whenever it fits the moment.

TIME

Physically here and now.

AUTHOR'S NOTES

Translations of Finnish sentences are inside double parentheses (((...))).

Nena has to come from far enough away to make her journey long and delicious. She is always in a panic when she comes from her apartment. Her walking takes so much of her energy that it would be no wonder that she, along the way, forgets what was in her mind. The audience must see her face, and she should come from a spot that isn't in Laura's and Tommi's sight, like from behind.

(*An atrium of a white condominium from the mid-century. Looks like a place where Marilyn went to rehab. Everything looks worn out, but there's a lot of white and cold, spring-like light.* **LAURA** *and* **TOMMI** *have moved to America five months ago.* **LAURA** *is sitting outside with* **TOMMI**, *only* **TOMMI**'s *schoolbooks and some papers are on a table with some pencils.* **LAURA** *is reading* **TOMMI**'s *school assignments. A very everyday situation.* **TOMMI** *is quiet, not participating. Here and there* **LAURA** *waits for him to answer, gives him moments when he could reply, but he doesn't say anything.*)

LAURA. Here, uhm, Jack went fishing. He had five worms in a can. This is a can. And three worms in his pocket. (*taps her pocket to show what is a pocket*) You have to draw his worms. This is a worm.

>(**TOMMI** *doesn't draw.*)

How many worms has he altogether? If you have five worms here in this can, and three in the pocket. Five plus three.

>(**TOMMI** *looks down.* **LAURA** *draws the answers.*)

Eight. Right? Jack put a new worm on his hook

>(*A weak, sad cry from on of the apartments.* **LAURA** *stops and listens for a second.*)

…after every fish he caught. He has two worms left. How many fish did he get?

>(**NENA** *appears from her and Geoff's apartment, very upset and seeking someone or something, notices* **LAURA** *and* **TOMMI** *but they don't notice her,* **LAURA** *keeps on talking.* **NENA** *starts to*

approach slowly and inevitably; first in panic, then forgetting what she had to say, then gradually getting happier on her way towards them.)

LAURA. He had eight worms here. Now he has two worms left. How many fish did he catch, if he got a fish with every worm? Eight minus two. Come on. I'll just draw it in here, and you draw the answer. It's not a language. It's only numbers.

    *(**LAURA** draws the equation to the paper.)*

Please try.

    *(**TOMMI** doesn't write.)*

I'm not going to give up. I'm sorry. You are only going to hear English –

NENA. Hola!

LAURA. Hello, Nina.

NENA. Well who is this gorgeous little boy? Hello!

    *(**TOMMI** is curious about **NENA**.)*

Is he your nephew? What a beautiful little boy.

LAURA. He is my son.

NENA. He is your son?

LAURA. Nina, you know he's my son. We're doing his homework. It's too hot inside.

    *(**MR. DORROS** is rehearsing fragments of a piano piece in one of the apartments.)*

NENA. Is he the only one?

LAURA. Yes.

NENA. *(to **TOMMI**)* You're gorgeous.

    *(**TOMMI** carefully agrees that he might very well be whatever she's saying.)*

Will you get married some day?

    *(**TOMMI** looks at his mom with a question mark.)*

Can I come to your wedding?

(TOMMI and NENA both stare at each other in an attracted awe.)

NENA. I'm going to Paris.

LAURA. Very nice. Have a nice journey to Paris.

(NENA stands still looking at TOMMI. LAURA is waiting for NENA to realize she should perhaps leave. TOMMI is waiting for NENA to continue talking. LAURA is the first one to give up and breaks the silence.)

We could continue doing his homework.

(NENA isn't going anywhere. TOMMI looks at NENA, NENA looks at TOMMI, LAURA looks at them.)

Why don't – why don't you write Nina's name, Tommi.

(TOMMI looks at his mom. He knows what LAURA's trying, but wants to do it for NENA.)

"N." "I."

NENA. It's "e."

LAURA. What?

NENA. It's N-E-N-A. But people never write it right here in America so here I'm just Nina.

(TOMMI has written "Nena" on the paper and gives it to her.)

Thank you honey. You know Geoff, my husband, taught the Cuban kids during the big migration.

LAURA. I remember. Geoff told us.

NENA. The best way to teach English to immigrants is total immersion.

(NENA feels weird after mentioning Geoff.)

LAURA. That's what I'm trying to do. Nobody has heard him say a word in English and we've been living here for five months already.

NENA. *(to* **TOMMI,** *with sadness)* You're gorgeous. *(turns and starts to walk away towards her apartment)*

LAURA. You could practice with Nena. You could try talking English with her. Do you know why?

TOMMI. *(shakes his head)*

LAURA. She has Alzheimer's. Do you know what that is?

> (**TOMMI** *thinks for a while, then nods.*)

Every time you have that same conversation, you could try different sentences on her. She won't remember. She will forget it.

> *(They watch* **NENA** *go.* **LAURA** *turns back to the school books. Mispronounces some of the sharks. Continues to read them until* **NENA** *has reached the apartment and we hear her weak cry.)*

There are about three hundred sixty-eight different species of shark which are divided into thirty families. Grey reef shark. Hammerhead shark. Nurse shark. Bonnethead shark. Porbeagle shark. Pygmy shark. Great white shark.

> *(A weak, sad cry from* **NENA**'s *apartment.* **LAURA** *and* **TOMMI** *think they heard something and listen to the wind for a second.* **MR. DORROS** *is playing the piano.)*

TOMMI. Äiti? *((Mom?))*

LAURA. Call me "Mom."

TOMMI. Enkä. *((Will not.))*

LAURA. "Mom."

TOMMI. Eiku "äiti." *((No, it's "mom."))*

> (**NENA** *reappears from her and Geoff's apartment, very upset and seeking someone, notices* **LAURA** *and* **TOMMI,** *and starts to approach slowly but inevitably. She tries hard to remember what she*

has to say, but again forgets. Looking at **TOMMI** *makes her get happier on her way towards them.)*

LAURA. *(Reading from a book, mutters.* **NENA**'s *approaching.)* Manta ray. Whale shark. Tresher shark. Wobbegong – wob – wobbygone – shark. This is too hard for children. Wobbegong? Wabbeegang? Sharks can only swim forward. Most of the sharks never sleep. Sharks have existed for over three hundred fifty million years. They have evolved long before dinosaurs or humans did. There are three migratory patterns: Local sharks do not migrate. Coastal pelagic sharks can migrate over 1000 miles. Highly pelagic sharks can migrate across oceans.

NENA. *(with all the sunshine and happiness in the world)* Hola! Well hello! Who's this little boy? What's your name?

> **(LAURA** *waits for* **TOMMI** *to answer.* **TOMMI** *is very interested in* **NENA**, *but doesn't answer.)*

LAURA. His name is Tommi. *(teaching* **TOMMI***)* My name is Tommi.

NENA. Your name is also Tommi?

LAURA. No, I was just teaching him. No, no, my name is Laura. You know that.

NENA. You don't live here.

LAURA. Yes we do. We moved here five months ago. We are your neighbors.

NENA. *(to* **TOMMI***)* Aren't you gorgeous.

TOMMI. Mitä se sano, äiti? *((What did she say, Mom?))*

LAURA. It's "What did she say, Mom?"

NENA. What? I'm not your mom.

LAURA. No, no. He is my son.

NENA. You're his mother?

LAURA. Yes, I'm his mother.

NENA. *(to* **TOMMI***)* Will you invite me to your wedding?

TOMMI. (*Turns to* **LAURA**, *wanting to know what* **NENA** *said.* **LAURA** *will not translate because he is speaking Finnish.*) Mitä se sano? ((*What'd she say?*))

NENA. We'll dance right here on this yard. There will be music and you will dance with Nena, won't you, little boy?

LAURA. Is Geoff at home, Nina?

TOMMI. (*correcting his mom*) Nena.

NENA. Geoff is my husband you know. He's mine.

LAURA. Of course he's yours.

NENA. (*turns her attention to* **LAURA** *at full force, suddenly very jealous*) You're beautiful.

LAURA. Thank you.

> (**TOMMI** *is trying very hard to follow what the women are talking about.*)

TOMMI. Mitä se sano? Äiti mitä se sano? ((*What'd she say? Mom what'd she say?*))

NENA. I used to be beautiful. Geoff says I looked like Sophia Loren. Well not so much anymore. Where's your husband?

> (*This was an unpleasant question for* **LAURA**.)

Geoff is mine. Don't you take him away from me.

LAURA. Nobody's gonna take him away from you.

NENA. You leave my husband alone, fucking bitch.

LAURA. You should leave us alone now. (*very firmly*) Go. Now.

> (**NENA** *starts to retreat slowly.*)

TOMMI. (*very worried*) Sanoiksä sille rumasti? ((*Were you rude to her?*))

LAURA. It's ok, she won't remember. She's just probably hungry. Don't talk in Finnish. Read from here.

> (*Pushes the book towards* **TOMMI**. **TOMMI** *is so frustrated he just throws the book away and shouts out loud.*)

TOMMI. Tyhmä paskanaama! Mä en lue mitään! *((Stupid shitface! I'm not reading anything!!))*

> *(TOMMI wants to go after NENA. LAURA stops him.)*

LAURA. We are never going back home.

> *(TOMMI freezes.)*

Me ei koskaan palata kotiin. *((We are never going back home.))*

> *(TOMMI looks like he has been run into the ground.)*

(Gathering herself. We hear piano practicing.) Hear that? Mr Dorros is practicing his piano even though he is a grown up already. *(Tries to get back to the homework. She seems tired and tense.)* Here you have to circle real or make-believe. The sky is falling. Is that real or make-believe?

> *(TOMMI doesn't circle.)*

> *(NENA doesn't quite make it into her home this time. A weak, sad cry bursts out from her mouth when she remembers why she keeps coming out of their apartment. She turns back and starts to walk towards LAURA and TOMMI, walking painfully slowly, trying very hard to remember, so she mumbles to herself:)*

NENA. Geoff, Geoff, Geoff, Geoff...

LAURA. The sky *(points to the sky)* is falling *(shows "falling" with her hand)*. Is that real? Or is it make-believe? Is the sky falling down or is it up there, not really falling down?

NENA. ...Geoff, Geoff...

LAURA. It is make-believe. The sky is not falling. The sky is up there. Circle this one. Make-believe.

NENA. *(reaches LAURA and TOMMI, is about to speak)*

> *(TOMMI stands up.)*

TOMMI. Hola, Nena.

NENA. No, it's Geoff –

TOMMI. *(has great difficulties in saying:)* My name is Tommi.

> (**TOMMI** *and* **NENA** *look at each other, a smile comes to* **NENA***'s face.* **LAURA** *is astonished.*)

NENA. *(has now totally forgotten what she had to say about Geoff)* Look at this gorgeous little boy! You're gorgeous! Look at you!

TOMMI. *(with a lot of effort)* Thank you.

> (**TOMMI** *and* **NENA** *stand and look at each other with great interest.*)

NENA. Is this your mother?

TOMMI. No.

LAURA. Yes, I am. I'm his mother.

TOMMI. Sä oot mun *äiti*. *(You're my **mom**.)*

NENA. Will you get married some day?

TOMMI. Yees.

NENA. Will you invite me to your wedding?

TOMMI. Yees.

> *(Points at the note he wrote, with* **NENA***'s name on it,* **NENA** *is holding the paper in her hand.)*

NENA. What's this?

LAURA. It's your name.

NENA. It's my name?

LAURA. Tommi wrote it down for you.

NENA. So you already invited me?

TOMMI. Yees.

NENA. I'm going to Paris. Could you give me a kiss, Tommi?

> (**TOMMI** *goes near* **NENA** *and kisses her on the cheek twice.* **NENA** *holds his hands.*)

There's gonna be music. And you invited me and we'll dance.

TOMMI. Yees.

NENA. Geoff won't come.

(Music starts to play.)

LAURA. *(looks to* **NENA**'s *and Geoff's apartment, worried)* OK, I'm gonna let you dance for a while, Tommi.

NENA. Geoff already went to Paris.

> *(The music is playing.* **NENA** *and* **TOMMI** *are dancing.* **LAURA** *approaches* **NENA**'s *and Geoff's apartment.* **NENA** *drops the note with her name on it. Darkness.)*

The Battle of Coney Island

David Jacobi

THE BATTLE OF CONEY ISLAND was first produced by Theater Masters (Julia Hansen, Artistic Director; Naomi McDougall Jones, Associate Artistic Director/Managing Director) in New York City on April 28, 2015. The performance was directed by Taylor Haven Holt. The cast was as follows:

THOMAS EDISON.......................................Bob Jaffe
NICOLA TESLA.......................................Jim Bergwall

CHARACTERS

THOMAS EDISON – 60s. Inventor. Businessman.
NICOLA TESLA – 50s. Inventor.

SETTING

Heaven.

CHARACTERS

THOMAS EDISON – 60s. Inventor. Businessman.
NICOLA TESLA – 50s. Inventor.

SETTING

Heaven.

(**THOMAS EDISON** *is sitting at a table. He's waiting. He sips water. He waits. There is a familiarity to it. He's comfortable. This is not his home, but it's kind of like if he decided to take his shoes and socks off, no one would feel weird about it.*)

(**EDISON** *stands up, puts his hands behind his back, and wanders around.*)

(**NICOLA TESLA** *walks in and sits down. He drinks some of his water. He thinks about a conversation he just had.* **EDISON** *makes a gesture as if to say, "Well?"*)

TESLA. The elephant isn't coming.

EDISON. Why not?

TESLA. She's just not coming. She adamantly refuses to join us.

EDISON. Oh, well. I tried. Did she give a reason?

TESLA. …

"Confusion."

EDISON. "Confusion?"

TESLA. She says she's not coming because she's still "extremely confused."

EDISON. About what?

TESLA. What do you think?

She said to me, and I am just paraphrasing,

"Since arriving here, I have spent a significant amount of my time here inquiring about the circumstances surrounding my untimely death, and although many have been gracious and patient enough to attempt to clarify the motives and reasoning behind Thomas

Edison's actions, no one has been able to tell me... why he did it."

Okay, so... I'm going to go/

> (**EDISON** *turns around once, throwing his arms in the air.*)

EDISON. I ALREADY TOLD HER WHY/

> (**TESLA** *waves a little, looking for a moment to leave.*)

TESLA. /I KNOW! GOOD/BYE

EDISON. /ONE OF THE FIRST THINGS I DID WHEN I GOT HERE WAS TELL THAT ELEPHANT WHY I KILLED HER

I had just gotten here. And she charges RIGHT AT ME

And I was nonplussed! I had never dreamed that this confrontation would occur at all, let alone so soon after my arrival! And then she says to me, in a very demanding, UNCOMFORTABLY LOUD voice/

TESLA. *(realizing that he's stuck)* /Yeah, I imagine it would have been loud/

EDISON. /She says to me, "Hey! Edison! What was *that* all about?"

> *(making a hold on gesture)*

I told her, "It was out of my hands! You killed three of your trainers, your life was forfeit!"

TESLA. Well, that's not entirely truthful/

EDISON. /Yes, I admit, I actually didn't care if she killed a man or not, I was planning to kill her anyway, but I wasn't about to say that to her/

TESLA. /She's an elephant/

EDISON. /I told her that her life was forfeit and in response she says,

"Yes, *but*...since I was not executed for my crime but instead sold to you, an unrelated party, my death sentence should have been pardoned, or at the very least, commuted."

I decided to keep my mouth shut and not dismantle *that* bullshit argument but instead of recognizing my silence as discomfort and politely changing the subject, she presses on and asks, "Did you kill me so you can eat me? I have seen that done before" to which I replied,

"Ew, no, human beings don't eat elephants, for some reason that seems disgusting."

TESLA. I imagine she took that poorly/

EDISON. /SHE TOOK THAT *SO* POORLY. You'd think she would have been willing to let bygones be bygones if I, after murdering her, would have eaten her corpse, right on the Coney Island Boardwalk/

TESLA. /You would have needed help.

EDISON. Huh?

TESLA. Eating her. Her body was…that…of an elephant. There's no way you could have eaten an entire elephant on your own.

You would have needed the assistance of… *(thinking, doing complex math)* eighty-three people.

> *(Beats. **EDISON** just stares at **TESLA**, thinking "What the hell is wrong with you?")*

EDISON. Are you done/

TESLA. /Yes, I'm done/

EDISON. /And then she's all like, "If you didn't want to eat me, then why, Edison? Why did you kill me? And so I told her. I said, "My dear Topsy, I killed you because it was part of a larger plot to ruin another man. Murdering you was a way of discrediting my rival, because your death made him appear untrustworthy and slightly less intelligent than myself."

> *(**TESLA** slowly backs away, trying to make a quiet exit.)*

She just stared at me after that.

Right through me. Right to my *bones*. I had to leave without saying goodbye.

(**EDISON** *turns around.* **TESLA** *stops trying to leave.*)

EDISON. She really declined?

TESLA. Yes. Disrespectfully/

EDISON. /WWWWHAT?

TESLA. She actually made a point to say that. "I *disrespectfully* decline."

EDISON. Has anyone ever even *used* that phrase before? "I disrespectfully decline?" Does that even work as a *sentence*/

TESLA. /Nope/

EDISON. /Elephants are willfully ignorant of the laws of etiquette/

TESLA. /They don't care/about

EDISON. /But apparently they're keenly aware of the ins and outs of our criminal justice system.

"My sentence should have been pardoned, or at the very least, commuted."

HA

I almost did *that*, by the way

I almost laughed right in her elephant face when she said that but that would been extremely rude, considering… I, you know…

electrocuted her to death on the Coney Island boardwalk in front of an audience

(**TESLA** *doesn't like being reminded of that. He goes to leave, not caring about being rude. Meanwhile,* **EDISON** *throws up his hands, maybe gets up and paces around.*)

That elephantine bitch! All I want to do is make amends!

"I disrespectfully decline." She's the worst.

(**TESLA** *is now gone.*)

Also, whose idea was it to make people heaven and elephant heaven THE SAME THING?

(Because he thinks **EDISON** *is wrong,* **TESLA** *comes back to let him know. It's a compulsion.)*

TESLA. Nope, you're wrong, it's all the same heaven/

EDISON. No it's not/

TESLA. /Yes it is. There are dogs and tortoises and sea cucumbers and rabbits up here/

EDISON. /There are no bees, Tesla. No bees.

TESLA. Yes there are

EDISON. Where are the bees? Tell me where you've seen bees.

*(***TESLA*** thinks.)*

TESLA. You're right. There are no bees. Where do you think they've gone?

EDISON. To hell, of course.
They took me down there, before bringing me up here showed me how close I was to going there instead
Bee Heaven is People Hell.

(Beats.)

TESLA. Maybe People Heaven is Elephant Hell.

EDISON. That is out of line, Tesla.

TESLA. Not it's not. Maybe Topsy's in hell for her transgressions against man
maybe hell is knowing your killer is somewhere nearby, always wanting an audience with you.

EDISON. No, Elephant Hell isn't People Heaven, it's Poacher Heaven/

TESLA. /No, it only works the other way with Poacher Hell being Elephant Heaven
Poacher Heaven is Tiger Hell/

EDISON. /Tiger Hell is Monkey Heaven/

TESLA. /What? Why? If anything, Monkey Heaven is Banana Hell, not/

EDISON. /Banana Hell is Fruit Fly Heaven, you idiot/

TESLA. /You know, it's probably just "Fruit Heaven," not different heavens for different fruit/

EDISON. /Then where do tomatoes go/

TESLA. /I'm not getting into this with you/

> (**EDISON** *goes to put his hand on* **TESLA***'s shoulder.*)

EDISON. (*in a way that lets us know* **EDISON** *is enjoying this a little*) /Yes you are

> (**TESLA** *recoils from* **EDISON***'s incoming touch.*)

TESLA. /YES I AM, AND I'M GOING TO WIN!
tomatoes are vegetables and Vegetable Hell is Salad Heaven and Salad Hell is Vinegar Heaven which is Oil Hell which is Fire Heaven which is also Hatred Heaven and
I HATE YOU! I hate you so much and you love this you always have
maybe Edison Heaven is Tesla Hell.
Now, can I go?

EDISON. You don't want to work this out?

TESLA. There's nothing to work out.
you had no right doing what you did to me
Topsy was right. You're a son of a bitch.
You lied and you cheated and you tried to ruin me.

EDISON. Well, you were winning. What was I supposed to do?

> (*A beat.* **TESLA** *looks at* **EDISON**.)

TESLA. Lose.

> (**EDISON** *lets that sink in for only a brief moment.*)

EDISON. You are so...goddamn un-American it hurts sometimes/

TESLA. /I'm American/

EDISON. You're an Armenian dickhead/

TESLA. I'm Serbian/

EDISON. /You're a Serbian dickhead, Tesla.

> I don't care what your Ellis Island paperwork says
> If you were a *real* American, you'd know that I couldn't just *lose*
> Did Washington Lose? No. Did Ben Franklin lose? No. Did General Custer lose/

TESLA. /Yes.

EDISON. He died before he could lose; it doesn't count.
> And why are you even still sore about this?
> I distinctly remember you coming out on top that day
> I could have killed a thousand elephants on the Coney Island boardwalk and it wouldn't have done any good/

TESLA. /Then how come you left a legacy that will last through the next civilization, while I died alone in a shithole flophouse?

*(A beat. **EDISON** shrugs. A beat. **TESLA** exits.)*

EDISON. It was you!

*(**TESLA** comes back.)*

> If you want the truth; it was you.
> Yeah, you were brilliant. You were even better than me. Maybe. I don't know, I'm sure some people have said that.
> But in the end, you beat you.

TESLA. Well, you didn't make things any easier.

EDISON. ...no. I didn't.
> I'm, uh… I'm sorry. I'm so sorry, Nick.

*(**EDISON** sticks out his hand for a handshake. **TESLA** wants to shake his hand, but he can't. Something deep inside stops him. Fear in his eyes.)*

*(**TESLA** tries to take it. He trembles.)*

EDISON. Just take it, you goddamn weirdo.

*(**TESLA** tries to do it, but can't. He actually lifts his arms to strangle **EDISON**, as he's always wanted to do that. He stops himself from doing it. He tries to*

> *shake his hand again, but he can't. He gives up in frustration.)*

TESLA. How is it more difficult than when I was alive? Seems unfair, doesn't it?

All this time, same as it ever was; Tesla Heaven is Tesla Hell.

> *(A beat. **EDISON** decides to offer both of his hands, in the pose of a dance.)*
>
> *(**TESLA** sees this as something a little easier to do. He takes **EDISON**'s hands. They begin to dance.)*

EDISON. I wish the elephant would finally come. I truly wish it.

…

I killed her, Nick.

TESLA. I know.

EDISON. I've got things too I want to say to her. I truly do.

Truly.

Maybe something resembling an apology.

TESLA. I know.

> *(Eventually, music joins them. Somewhere in heaven, an elephant plays a slow song.)*
>
> *(**EDISON** feels shame, self-pity, but then a current of forgiveness. He smiles. **TESLA** never smiles.)*

End of Play

Nordic Ambition (Self Portrait #3)

Phillip Howze

NORDIC AMBITION (SELF PORTRAIT #3) was first produced by Theater Masters (Julia Hansen, Artistic Director; Naomi McDougall Jones, Associate Artistic Director/Managing Director) in New York City on April 28, 2015. The performance was directed by Margot Bordelon. The cast was as follows:

SUSPENDED MAN................................... Jelani Alladin

CHARACTERS

SUSPENDED MAN – Male, African-American, 30s, heavyset
THE MOVIE STAR – Female or male, African-American, any age (*offstage*)

NOTE

Punctuation, or lack thereof
Someone once called this play "a verbal slalom"
In production, we discovered a lot in working *without subtext*

Press play on the audio marked: VID00197.AVI

THE MOVIE STAR. *(sound projected)*
"Okay, because I'm a wimp I had to be taken down on the sleigh ok
That's what's happening to me right now"

(snow sounds)

"Ugh"

(wind sounds)

*(***THE MOVIE STAR** *pants)*

*(***THE MOVIE STAR** *pants)*

Lights up

A black man in a wet snow suit

A large, wet sled and skis

All are suspended, hanging in midair

Press pause on the audio

SUSPENDED MAN.
There was
an um ah treatise written on thee,
nature of embarrassment and I'm not sure who wrote that but
he was a man probably. Ahm pretty sure uh that. Andnd,
about embarrassment was wrote something, something
to do with shame, or rather, public –

You can when you youre younger or, I could I could
shield myself
from shame and by mommy or being
really mean or combative
back towards someone who was fun making fun
or making – ha ha –

ha at it, but, that's not was that auto-defensive
or just Being
you know um? Mean.

We should do things about things before
We die.
Bucket list things methinks
But uhman adult man without money does
remembers things like
wipe outs on the winter Olympics anded
the the tragic death
of Natasha Richardson
can be frightened
of sharing those memories a little
ashamed perhapsing
that unnecessary death happens when you least expectant
or could that happen to you? Man.
Or woman.

> *He screams*
>
> *A sudden, two-second flash of bright light*
>
> *It flashes onto the hanging body before disappearing*

But sounds like something a woman also maybe
could have written also about.
Women are too often too embarrassed
by things which is is not to say today that women are
ahm
generally overembarrassed, but. But
bubt perhaps harassed by men. Like me
Memory of embarrassshame. In front of their kids.
For in front of their kids And their adults. And
And kids.
Are – ha ha –
Standing at about, mmmm, ahhmuh quarter of my age

NORDIC AMBITION (SELF PORTRAIT #3)

Or more are there
standing up on the kiddie slope skiing standing up
Not sitting down Not a care in the world Nor a cry.
Orm embarrassmented
Or ahm having to explain themselves to strangers or
come up for air
Are reasons as to why theyre here
in this neighborhood falling down. No
not care-filled or uncaring or nor shy of life's
little inexperiences
and nn that's how it happens when you cease.
For shame, they say. For shame.

Are they – did she that 8 year-old 18 year-old did she
just just
laugh at me and my – state of waiting?
I can't Was that a smile, or, a grimace?? No.
Not no she's pointing at
And laughing at my – Is she? That little bitch. – that little
Is she?

> *He screams*
>
> *A sudden, four-second flash of bright light*
>
> *It flashes onto the hanging body before disappearing*

You could and I may think of myself as a
Black double-diamond, but
Sometimes you have to laugh at it At times
you have to accept your position as a green ring.

There are things you shoulda and shouldnta as in
some bucket list stuffs like that what harmed
other people in the doing. Like that.
Smoking. Like child-rearing-bearing.
Buying candy.

Or whistling at fine women That's that.
This is a mountain I'm on.
I was never meant to be pregnant or up here or, ambitious.
Could somebody's God have saved me? Or the government?
– ha ha –
People are alive, until they dead. Suddenly right where.
On ski slopes. In residential neighborhoods.
In but tomorrow what about that, I don't know many people but they'll soon know me. I bet.
I bet I don't know why I'm doing up so ascended but
How did we get here?
I guess it's that's my bad for leaving the house today.
– ha ha –
Having a sweet tooth.
Ha Hip-hop.
And I can imagine what theyll think, through that grimace.
Andespecially mommy
and mmm Martin Luther King Jr.
And him his thinking son – That wasn't the mountaintop I was referring to.

> *He hums a Negro Spirtual*
>
> *Perhaps "Go Tell It on the Mountain"*
>
> *A sudden, five-second flash of bright light*
>
> *It flashes onto the hanging body before disappearing*
>
> *Press play on the paused audio*
>
> *Distorted, the audio underscores the remainder of the play*

Is this because I didn't vote?
Is this because I wasn't nice to somebody, Did I laugh ha far too much?
Once in my –?
Parents tell you never to be ashamed of

who you are and, of course, parents are often ashamed of
who they were, which kids can see n are pleased to discern.
And then its too late. To do things diffidently.
And I never learned to swim.
And I never hunted a wild boar.
And I never kayaked across the Atlantic Ocean.
And I never got to run for President of anything ever.
And I never lost spare change in the crack of my couch only to be glad to discover it there years later.
And I never dyed my hair pink or purple
And I never learned another language
And I never had a walk on role in a play
And I never woke up in time to join the rally
And I never sang a song to the person I loved
And I never lost my other virginity
And I never got married and I never had kids
And I never taught them the true meaning of Christmas
And I never quite cared enough to properly pronounce the name Dos-toe-v-sky
And I never had my mother's name tattooed on my arm
And I always thought spectacle was important
And I had a dream
And I thought I was fighting the good fight by professing I was fighting the good fight
And I never finished the final season of *True Blood*
And I rarely ever prayed to your God
And you were on the internet and your phone
And you couldn't sit still long enough to find spiritual balance in a meditative state
And you voted based on strategy and instead of on principles
And I kept thinking
And I kept thinking about tomorrow
Tomorrow will be the day I do it

Tomorrow will be the when I finish
Tomorrow will be when
Tomorrow will be, wont it?
Tomorrow I will
Tomorrow will
Tomorrow
Tomorrow
I'll love you tomorrow
And I never made it down the mountain
And I never made it round the bend
And I never made to the promised land
And I never made the news

–

–

–

Until today

> *The inaudible audio continues playing*
>
> *Lights dim cloaking the scene entirely in stark silhouette*
>
> *One minute*
>
> *The audio cuts abruptly*
>
> *The* **SUSPENDED MAN** *and the skis hang in silhouette*
>
> *Two minutes in silent suspension*

End of Play

Of Our Own

Matthew Capodicasa

OF OUR OWN was first produced by Theater Masters (Julia Hansen, Artistic Director; Naomi McDougall Jones, Associate Artistic Director/Managing Director) in New York City on April 28, 2015. The performance was directed by Margot Bordelon. The cast was as follows:

THEO .... Benjamin Harris
BECKY .... Naomi McDougall Jones

CHARACTERS

THEO – male, 30, any ethnicity. Grizzled, unkempt, dirty, wild and old eyes.

BECKY – female, 30, any ethnicity. Composed, a good listener, doesn't take crap.

AUTHOR'S NOTES

There are no chairs.

There are no props.

BECKY.	**THEO.**
I see him before he sees me	I see her before she sees me

BECKY. on a bench

THEO. in the park

BECKY. He turns / away

THEO. She turns away
She doesn't want / to see me.

BECKY. He doesn't want to see me.
He's shaking, he's so
cold.
So
thin.

THEO. She looks the same
but more sure of it.

BECKY. His clothes are soaked and caked
with mud and sweat and piss.

THEO. She's

BECKY. I'm

BECKY.	**THEO.**
sitting next to him.	sitting next to me.

THEO. She says

BECKY. I um
wasn't sure I was going to come over here.
He says

THEO. I have to be somewhere.

BECKY. Okay

THEO. I have an appointment.

BECKY. Alright

THEO. I'm needed
elsewhere.

BECKY. That's
  fine.

   ...

BECKY. His beard is
  He still can't really grow a
  It's actually kind of the neck beard I always worried
     about.
  He looks
  so hungry, it's
THEO. She says
BECKY. I tried to find you.
  I know that probably doesn't change anything or
  mean anything to you but
  For the first year after you left I
THEO. I know.
  Watched you.
BECKY. You watched me?
THEO. Best way to stay hidden
  is to watch who's searching for you.

   ...

BECKY. Is this where you
  sleep, or
THEO. Park closes.
  Have to leave.

   ...

BECKY. I'm not angry anymore.
THEO. She's still angry.
BECKY. When he moves
  the smell of urine
  refreshes itself.
THEO. She looks like

  she's been sucking on a lemon for the past five years.

She looks like
she eats kumquats.
She looks like
she's about to offer me money.

BECKY. You look hungry.

THEO.	**BECKY.**
I haven't eaten in two days.	
More than two days	*God*
Fifty-one and a half hours.	
Can't trust the food, it's	
all been	*Okay.*

    …

THEO. She's afraid of me.

BECKY. Theo

THEO. DON'T use that name.

    …

BECKY. How about a shower, then?
    You want a shower

THEO. Water supply
    Contaminated

BECKY. I'm trying to

THEO. Why don't you just
    offer me the cash in your wallet
    and leave me
    the fuck alone.

    …

BECKY. I want to.

THEO. She wants to

BECKY. But I can't I

THEO. But she can't, she

BECKY. Theo

THEO. *Don't use*

BECKY. SORRY I just
    What if we

THEO. Safe, this way.
    Safer, anyway.
    I know you don't see it and I know you don't *want* to see it but
BECKY. You're *starving*.
THEO. I KNOW.

    …

BECKY.	**THEO.**
Underneath the smell of	
urine, of	
body odor, of	
feet, of	She's
rotten milk, of	
garbage, of	Wearing the same perfume, it's
I think that's the	one smell it's many smells it's
That slightly	This plus this plus this plus this plus
cool	Her smiling barefoot
cozy	Reading at the table it's
smell of him?	Wearing my shirt from the hamper she'd
The	Smell like *us* it's
smell of him I used to	Smell like something I could
hide in	I might
The ocean, the ocean air, the	still fit into maybe, I

THEO. She is sad and
    it has always hurt me to know
    that when she is sad, I think she is
    the most beautiful.
BECKY. Please let me make you something.
    You can watch me cook it.

You can check all the ingredients, you
God, *please* / just
THEO. Okay
BECKY. What?
THEO. Okay.
>   *(Shift.)*

BECKY. We go back to my apartment.
THEO. You still live here.
BECKY. Yeah, I
THEO. You "hated it here," you
BECKY. I don't
THEO. She did, she
BECKY. He pads around the apartment
This tiny little slanty-floored apartment
that used to be his apartment and then our apartment and then my apartment.
He touches nothing.
He moves through the spaces where things used to be.
Things I've moved without even thinking.
Spaces I left empty for
THEO. She wants me to recognize
More than recognize, to *reclaim*
It's not that I don't recognize
It's that *owning* things means
BECKY. I'm seeing somebody.
THEO. Good.
BECKY. More than seeing We're getting married.
THEO. Where is he now?
BECKY. At work.
THEO. On a weekend.
BECKY. He's a lawyer.
THEO. Lawyers work weekends?
BECKY. Sometimes.

>   …

THEO. He doesn't live here.
BECKY. How do you know?
THEO. Just your smell.
No one else's.
Why doesn't he live here?
BECKY. I don't
Because
he doesn't.
I guess.

    …

BECKY. He goes to the bookshelf
and picks out
with this like enormous effort
one of his books
that I guess I
merged into *my* books
He opens to a page and reads
and laughs to himself
And breathes in, sharply.
That's the one you were reading
when you left.
Did you ever finish it?
THEO. No.
Still in
the middle.
And no one "left."
You made me go.
I just didn't come *back.*

    …

THEO. You see my parents at all?
BECKY. Not for
I guess about four years now.
Your mom, she

I don't know, she thought I killed you and hid the body or something.

I mean not for *long*, but there *was* like a two-day period where she kept calling me to threaten to call the police.

Your dad was here a lot, early on.

He stayed on the couch while he searched for you.

THEO. They couldn't
They wouldn't They wouldn't
SEE THE EVIDENCE THEY
I wrote them a letter.
After a year.

BECKY. They got it, they
They told me.
That's how I knew to
stop looking for you.

...

THEO. She wants
People want to understand but what they want is What they *want* is a way to
Call me Call me
A way to lock me up
A way to own me
A way to

BECKY. I um
have some tomatoes
That I grew out on the fire escape
Do you trust me to

THEO. Let me see.

BECKY. He takes the tomatoes.
Smells them.
Rubs them with his fingers
Fingers with dirt in his fingerprints.
Fingers of an old man.

...

BECKY. Please?
   Let me
THEO. These are fine.
   She slices the tomatoes.
   The knife it's
   It was mine.
   Those *words*:
   "Mine."
   "Yours."
   "Ours."
   They
BECKY. Theo, I'm so / sorry
THEO. *DON'T* use that name.
BECKY. *Sorry,* I / just want to
THEO. Is this tomato a
   condition of me like going to "see / someone"
BECKY. No, I
THEO. Fuck you.
   FUCK / YOU.
BECKY. Hey. HEY.
   This tomato is
   This tomato is a tomato.
   I'm not going to
   You can do what you want.

   …

THEO. I'm not showering.
BECKY. Okay.
THEO. The water supply is contaminated.
BECKY. Okay.
THEO. *Poison.*
BECKY. *Okay.*

   …

BECKY. He eats the tomato.

Delicately.
Calmly.
Elegantly.
Like he's not *starving*.

　　…

BECKY. I was trying to help you.
　Making you go, I was trying to *help* you.
　I didn't understand, if I'd *understood*

THEO. Then what?
　You'd have felt more guilty when you did the same exact thing?

BECKY. I

THEO. She's not crying.
　She won't cry.

BECKY. I wouldn't have made you
　go
　when you
　were in the middle of that book.

　　…

THEO. She wants
BECKY. I want
THEO. so badly
BECKY. so badly
　to say your name.

THEO. Don't.
　You *want*
　to forget me.

BECKY. I do not.
　I absolutely do not.
　Why do you think I'm still here
　in this terrible fucking overpriced slanted shitty apartment?
　So you can

THEO. Come back?
BECKY. Find a way
   back, yes.
   Not to me, but to
THEO. To what?

     …

THEO. Thank you for the tomato.
BECKY. He starts to leave
THEO. Will you tell the lawyer about me?
BECKY. No.
THEO. Because
BECKY. Because he
   Because that would hurt you.
THEO. Even you don't know what hurts and what helps.
   No one does.
BECKY. You could teach me.
   You could teach me to help you.
THEO. You think *I* You think You think
   that *I* have some idea of
   If I knew how to
   fix
   the *water supply*, I'd
BECKY. He starts to / cry.
THEO. Crying doesn't scare her.

BECKY.	**THEO.**
I won't turn away.	She won't turn away.
I'm afraid that if I	She's afraid of me and she
look away, he'll	looks at me.

THEO. She starts to cry.
   I need to / get out.
BECKY. He's out the door.
   I watch him / run down the street.
THEO. Run run run run run until I can breathe in the free
BECKY. And I see the

THEO. open / air
BECKY. air vibrate behind him.
   Leaving the trail
THEO. Until I don't smell her.
BECKY. Evidence of his being there / until
THEO. Until I can disappear Until she can
BECKY. Until I
THEO. forget me
BECKY. forget him
BECKY & THEO. Which is
BECKY. what scares him
THEO. what scares her
BECKY & THEO. most of all.

End of Play

Off Tackle Glide

Sean David DeMers

OFF TACKLE GLIDE was first produced by Theater Masters (Julia Hansen, Artistic Director; Naomi McDougall Jones, Associate Artistic Director/Managing Director) in New York City on April 28, 2015. The performance was directed by Joseph Ward. The cast was as follows:

ADAM .... Jelani Alladin
FATHER JAMES .... Bob Jaffe

CHARACTERS

ADAM – African-American College Football Player, 21
FATHER JAMES – Catholic Priest, 40

SETTING

Catholic Church; Present Day; Afternoon

AUTHOR'S NOTES

(/) – The next character's line starts and overlaps after this symbol.

(A church, a row or rows of benches with kneeling pad, votive candle table stage right, the audience is the sanctuary. **ADAM**, *21, is sitting on a pew and facing the audience, head bowed. He is nicely dressed, khakis and button shirt, with a ball cap in his back pocket and a plastic lanyard around his neck. There is a football behind him, hidden from the audience.)*

*(***FATHER JAMES***, 40, enters and heads to the votive table for maintenance.)*

FATHER JAMES. Good afternoon.

ADAM. It's afternoon now?

FATHER JAMES. Just after.

ADAM. Oh. Thanks.

Are you the priest here?

FATHER JAMES. Well, this is my branch office so to speak. I'm Father James.

ADAM. Oh? Cool.

(After a pause, in rhythm.)

Father James, Father James. Unh. Father James. Ease my pains, ease my pains. Unh. Father James.

FATHER JAMES. Does something pain you, Mr – ?

ADAM. Mister – ? Oh. Just call me Adam.

FATHER JAMES. Like the first man?

ADAM. I guess. Yeah. Someone's gotta be first, right?

FATHER JAMES. That's the way of things, especially for St. Thomas.

ADAM. Yeah…that St. Thomas, man. Yeah.

FATHER JAMES. Thomas Aquinas.

ADAM. You think I don't know?

FATHER JAMES. I didn't mean to insinuate / that you didn't –

ADAM. But actually…in actuality, I think you did mean to insinuate, am I right?

FATHER JAMES. I suppose so. Sorry, you got me.

ADAM. I know Aquinas. He said events, like creating the Earth, don't just happen they're put into motion. And God is the first mover – he was dumb, right?

FATHER JAMES. Well, he was misunderstood; quiet and thoughtful. They called him a "dumb ox."

ADAM. Dumb ox, yeah I read that. I think that's more interesting anyway. *Thinking* he's dumb. I like to know people's thoughts.

FATHER JAMES. When it comes to our own thoughts, we are the first movers; the imagination is the link between the corporeal and the spiritual. Adam, are you Catholic?

ADAM. I don't know. I don't know what I am.

FATHER JAMES. You sound like a Catholic.

ADAM. Do I need to be Catholic to be here?

FATHER JAMES. No, not at all. Everyone's welcome. You're coming to the combine service tonight?

ADAM. Wait, do you know who I am?

FATHER JAMES. Should I?

ADAM. No. Unless you're a spy or something. Are you a spy or something?

FATHER JAMES. No.

ADAM. Why do you know I'm a player?

FATHER JAMES. Adam, you know, you still have on your lanyard from the combine.

ADAM. Oh. That doesn't mean I'm a football player. Maybe I'm an agent.

FATHER JAMES. You're a little young for an agent and they don't usually tote these around.

*(He reaches behind **ADAM** and pulls out the football.)*

(**ADAM** *takes it.*)

ADAM. Maybe they do. Like, maybe I want to take a prospect by surprise, like I'm walking down the street and just say "heads up" and toss it at him.

(**ADAM** *tosses the ball to* **FATHER JAMES** *who catches it.*)

FATHER JAMES. To test reflexes?

ADAM. Reflex action is very important and if he catches it, boom, I sign him.

FATHER JAMES. Sounds like as good a method as any.

ADAM. It's the only method. So yeah, I'm a pretty big deal. I work in football, the NFL, the big show!

FATHER JAMES. Yeah, me too.

ADAM. What? Don't lie now. Look around, we're in a church here.

FATHER JAMES. I work for Green Bay.

ADAM. No way. You know Aaron Rodgers?

FATHER JAMES. I see him all the time.

ADAM. Whoa! That's important. I didn't know any teams had God on their side. Maybe the NFL's not so bad after all. I might think about signing with those guys.

FATHER JAMES. I thought you were an agent.

ADAM. Oh, well –

FATHER JAMES. Before you talk in circles, let me remind *you* to look around. You're in a church.

ADAM. You got me. Hey, you're good! I like you. I'm gonna put those Packers on my list.

(*He gets out a pad and pen and jots down a note.*)

FATHER JAMES. You know, this is the eighth year I've had this service and you're the first player I've seen. They're usually too busy.

ADAM. It's no big deal, just the psych day. I can't do a psych day when I'm not right, you know? I can't focus today. So I'm here to find peace. I gotta get right up here.

FATHER JAMES. It's nice to see a player have priorities that extend beyond football. I'd be willing to bet that plenty of owners would see your spiritual devotion as more important than a psychological test.

ADAM. Father – are you recruiting me?

FATHER JAMES. Ha! No, that would be a first though. "Priest signs new...quarterback?"

ADAM. Close, running back –

FATHER JAMES. Of course.

ADAM. – and stranger things have happened. You'd probably take ten percent of that!

FATHER JAMES. Fifteen, but I'd give it all to charity.

ADAM. Yeah. Cool. Green Bay would be nice, but I guess I'm supposed to be drafted by the Seahawks.

FATHER JAMES. Really? You've talked to them?

ADAM. Well, not directly – it sounds crazy, but – I had this dream. It was so clear. Seattle takes me 'cause they need a backup R.B. They take me late in the first and I shake some hands and they give me the number eight. It's all about the numbers – eight's my lucky number.

FATHER JAMES. That came to you in a dream?

ADAM. In great detail, Father; I'm so glad to get this off my chest, you know? I can't tell anyone else cause they'll think I'm nuts. Tell me something: What's it like working in the NFL?

FATHER JAMES. I'm doing what I love to do, what I've always loved, but now I have a sideline pass on top of it.

ADAM. Come on, I'm being serious now – is there something more? I need to know.

FATHER JAMES. I haven't really thought about it. It's unexplainable, but at times my proximity to that sort of supreme physical human achievement is more spiritual than anything I can do in this building.

ADAM. Yeah. Wow. Unexplainable. Now that I've talked to you, I know I'm supposed to be here, to take a day and get my head straight. So far I've just been going through the motions – making lists and taking notes, you know? None of it feels real. None of it feels right. It's like when I was seventeen I was hit over the head with a baseball bat – right here on the side. They said I'd never play football again, but I did and it was because I took the time to get my head straight. Not only did I play again, I got better at it. Sometimes I glide. I glide through the defense, you know? I take the ball and start running and close my eyes and just let God guide me off the tackle. They wouldn't touch me – it's a blessed thing. Unexplainable, right?

FATHER JAMES. Right.

ADAM. But yesterday I was surrounded by agents and coaches talking me up and it all felt so fake, you know? So when I woke up today I'm thinking football's just a game, it's like pretend, I mean look at all these dudes with big money in the NFL just messing up. It affects you. So, what's my greater destiny? Can I actually better myself and inspire people by carrying the rock? It doesn't really make sense, I mean – it's confusing I guess. That's why I had to come here first – could you help me get a message to Him?

FATHER JAMES. We're talking to God right now.

ADAM. This is confidential?

FATHER JAMES. Completely.

ADAM. I mean, don't get me wrong father, but here I am in a church to escape and I'm talking to someone in the NFL. Everywhere I turn, there's another agent, another coach – you're biased and you don't even know it.

FATHER JAMES. Well, nobody's perfect. For what it's worth, I still come here to this pew down in front, just as you've come today. I kneel right here and I talk and He listens. And then I light a candle. It's never easy this trust, this faith – but He's listening. Go ahead, talk to Him.

ADAM. *(He kneels.)* God? I'm scared. I get confused – by people mostly – people who tell me I could be a star, and rich, and I could have everything now. I want more than anything to glide through the defense like usual, but not in a game – in life. This football stuff, it feels like a test, because yesterday – you know what it was? I didn't feel you. I only felt alone. I need you to tell me if you're testing me. If I go back to football, am I failing or fulfilling your will? Thank you. Amen.

(*to* **FATHER JAMES**)

That's the first time in my life I've asked for what I want. When do I get an answer?

FATHER JAMES. Your will is His will.

ADAM. I don't want to make the wrong choice.

FATHER JAMES. Adam listen, you skipped the combine and came here for a reason. You don't have to feel alone. Come to the service I have for coaches and scouts tonight.

ADAM. Wait a minute, coaches and scouts are gonna / be here?

FATHER JAMES. It's a strong community. I think you'll feel a / kinship.

ADAM. Why didn't you say that before? I thought this was a private place.

FATHER JAMES. It is. It's a sanctuary, a safe place.

ADAM. I know what a sanctuary is and this ain't it! I can't be around any coaches, man!

FATHER JAMES. Okay, I just thought I could help. You don't have to be / around anyone.

ADAM. You're from the Packers; they put you up to this. They probably got a jersey all ready for me.

FATHER JAMES. Nothing is further from the truth. Not many kids get this opportunity. You're here, what harm is there in going back and trying to figure out if you love football –

ADAM. I'm not feeling that. What if that advice is based on you not being able to hear me? People out there ain't listening, why should I expect people in here to listen?

FATHER JAMES. I'm listening – I meant it when I said your will is His will. It's okay to make a decision and then have faith in it. Do you know Psalm 37?

ADAM. …

FATHER JAMES. "Take delight in the Lord and He will give you the desires of your heart."

> *(A large door opens off.* **FATHER JAMES** *turns out to look as* **ADAM** *dives into his pocket and puts on his ball cap and a pair of sunglasses.* **ADAM** *rises as* **FATHER JAMES** *regards him.)*

ADAM. There's your coaches and agents.

FATHER JAMES. It's early still, and you didn't / light a candle.

ADAM. *(a little too loud)* Thanks father, thanks! I guess I'm not a Catholic after all, but you've been a big help!

FATHER JAMES. Adam, wait!

ADAM. Never heard of him. *(He removes his lanyard and drops it.)* I'm nobody. Who's this Adam?

FATHER JAMES. The first man.

ADAM. Someone's gotta be first, right?

> *(***FATHER JAMES*** picks up the lanyard as* **ADAM** *leaves. He crosses and begins to light a candle as the lights fade.)*

End of Play

Laodamiad

Chas LiBretto

LAODAMIAD was first produced by Theater Masters (Julia Hansen, Artistic Director; Naomi McDougall Jones, Associate Artistic Director/Managing Director) in New York City on April 28, 2015. The performance was directed by Joseph Ward. The cast was as follows:

LAODAMIA . . . . Kea Trevett
ACASTUS. . . . . Jim Bergwall
PROTESILAOS . . . . Benjamin Harris

CHARACTERS

LAODAMIA – Female, 20s
ACASTUS – Male, 50s to 60s
PROTESILAOS – Male, 20s

SETTING

Today or Yesterday. Ancient Thessaly or anywhere affected by war.

*(**ACASTUS** steps forward.)*

ACASTUS. There was a time
not long after they sent our men to Troy
When the war was in its early days
When we all thought it would be over by winter.
When we thought our boys would be home and safe within a few weeks.
When the leaders of the nations left it
for the gods to decide
how the lessons in grief would be taught.

(A knocking is heard on the door.)

*(We see **LAODAMIA**.)*

(There is worry on her face.)

(She nods her heads slowly.)

(She takes a step back.)

(She looks faint on her feet.)

(She begins to collapse to the floor.)

*(**ACASTUS** comes to her.)*

(He helps her up.)

(He carries her weight.)

(He holds her.)

LAODAMIA. Father…
He's –
My husband is –
He's not coming home –
from the war.
He's not coming home.

ACASTUS. I know.

LAODAMIA. He's never going to come home!

ACASTUS. No. He isn't.

LAODAMIA. They murdered him!!
Cruel Hector, those horrible Trojans –
My baby,
They took him from me.
I don't want to live if he's not here
I want to die too.

ACASTUS. No!
No, stay with me for a while, daughter.
Come home with me.

LAODAMIA. But I'm a grown-up, father.
I can't just move back into my old childhood room.
With all my childhood things.
I can't do that.

ACASTUS. Just for a little while.

(He turns out.)

Laodamia sank deeper and deeper into darkness that winter.
She tried to join her husband in death more than once.
But the gods had a plan.
The first Greek to die
Deserved a last goodbye.

*(**PROTESILAOS** gasps.)*

(He lurches upward, confused, pale and forlorn.)

PROTESILAOS. O
O
Oh!
O terror.
What hath she perceived?
O Joy
What doth she look on
Who doth she behold?

ACASTUS. Her hero slain upon the beach of Troy
Agony stared from his grey face.

> (**PROTESILAOS** *almost falls.*)
>
> (*It is as though he needs to learn to walk again.*)
>
> (**ACASTUS** *steadies him as they walk him to the house.*)

Just follow me as I lead you, son.
Come. What fears you a house
When you have faced death itself?

> (**LAODAMIA** *comes running out and embraces her husband.*)

LAODAMIA. Husband! Husband
I will never let you go again!

> (*She holds him but he does not respond with any emotion.*)

PROTESILAOS. I cannot stay long.

LAODAMIA. …
oh.
I thought…
I thought there was pity in this.
It was all…
so brief.

PROTESILAOS. Mortals are much deceived by groundless hopes.

LAODAMIA. You're so cold.

PROTESILAOS.
I have suffered
Such things as await you.
And every one.

LAODAMIA. What did it feel like?
…I'm sorry I wasn't there…

PROTESILAOS. Like I was filled with tiny holes
All leaking out everything important about me.

And the holes kept opening up
And I kept trying to plug them
But there were too many
And I was losing everything there was about me
Faster than I could think.
Faster than I could feel
Faster than I realized
Soon I was pouring out of myself,
I was coming out of the hole too
And I could see myself
But I was becoming far away
I was leaving myself.
Through the tiny holes.

>   (**ACASTUS** *shakes his head.*)

>   (*There is no dignity in this reunion.*)

ACASTUS. The gods are children,
to torment our hearts like this.

PROTESILAOS. Perhaps.
But they are still the gods.

LAODAMIA. Why did it happen this way.

PROTESILAOS. It was my duty.

LAODAMIA. Your duty?
Your duty to follow after that…
That Helen and –
There's no *reason* to it!

PROTESILAOS. Do you look for someone to blame?

LAODAMIA. Yes.

PROTESILAOS. Blame fate.
My thread was spun from the beginning.
…
My time is up.
Good bye.

LAODAMIA. But I'm not ready!

ACASTUS. Her hero slain upon the beach of Troy
Agony stared from his grey face.

>   *(**PROTESILAOS** almost falls.)*

>   *(It is as though he needs to learn to walk again.)*

>   *(**ACASTUS** steadies him as they walk him to the house.)*

Just follow me as I lead you, son.
Come. What fears you a house
When you have faced death itself?

>   *(**LAODAMIA** comes running out and embraces her husband.)*

LAODAMIA. Husband! Husband
I will never let you go again!

>   *(She holds him but he does not respond with any emotion.)*

PROTESILAOS. I cannot stay long.

LAODAMIA. …
oh.
I thought…
I thought there was pity in this.
It was all…
so brief.

PROTESILAOS. Mortals are much deceived by groundless hopes.

LAODAMIA. You're so cold.

PROTESILAOS.
I have suffered
Such things as await you.
And every one.

LAODAMIA. What did it feel like?
…I'm sorry I wasn't there…

PROTESILAOS. Like I was filled with tiny holes
All leaking out everything important about me.

And the holes kept opening up
And I kept trying to plug them
But there were too many
And I was losing everything there was about me
Faster than I could think.
Faster than I could feel
Faster than I realized
Soon I was pouring out of myself,
I was coming out of the hole too
And I could see myself
But I was becoming far away
I was leaving myself.
Through the tiny holes.

> (**ACASTUS** *shakes his head.*)

> (*There is no dignity in this reunion.*)

ACASTUS. The gods are children,
to torment our hearts like this.

PROTESILAOS. Perhaps.
But they are still the gods.

LAODAMIA. Why did it happen this way.

PROTESILAOS. It was my duty.

LAODAMIA. Your duty?
Your duty to follow after that…
That Helen and –
There's no *reason* to it!

PROTESILAOS. Do you look for someone to blame?

LAODAMIA. Yes.

PROTESILAOS. Blame fate.
My thread was spun from the beginning.
…
My time is up.
Good bye.

LAODAMIA. But I'm not ready!

PROTESILAOS. Who ever is?
  But my time is up.
LAODAMIA. Let me come with you.
PROTESILAOS. It may not be.
  It never has been.
ACASTUS. What good did this do?
PROTESILAOS. It was never my choice.
  Farewell.

> *(He goes.)*

> *(**LAODAMIA** stands center, lost in an ever-deepening fantasy.)*

ACASTUS. By that time,
  There were war memorials
  springing up in town centers,
  The war was being remembered
  Even as it was fought.
  The fallen remembered before they fell
  As plaques and statues.
LAODAMIA. I shall not forsake a loved one,
  even though he is lifeless.
PROTESILAOS. The weeks went by.
  I heard her speaking, one day
  The way I'd heard her sound
  before the war.
  She sounded happy.
  I liked hearing her that way.
  And I let her go on.

> *(Lights come up on a statue of **PROTESILAOS**.)*

> *(In actuality, the same actor as before, though standing still as death.)*

> *(**LAODAMIA** comes on, bright and cheerful with a hand-truck.)*

*(She scoops the **PROTESILAOS** statue onto it and then moves him over to a kitchen table.)*

(She serves the statue breakfast and coffee.)

LAODAMIA. ...the truth is...

I just don't think we knew each other that *well* when we got married.

We were so young.

We *are* so young.

Maybe we rushed.

We didn't know what we were getting ourselves into and...

No! Of course I want to stay married!

That isn't what I'm saying.

I want us to work *harder.*

To try to find again

Why we fell in love in the first place.

Let's use this as an opportunity!

Let's get to know each other again.

Let's go somewhere.

Let's go on *vacation*!

We didn't even have time for a honeymoon!

the truth is...

I just don't think we knew each other that *well* when we got married.

We were so young.

We *are* so young.

Maybe we rushed.

I still find you attractive!

Of course I do!

Please don't think I don't.

I think you're even more handsome now than you were then.

I'm not flattering you,

I really think that.

You have this glow.
This ethereal glow.
Maybe it's a tan?
Are you oiling yourself?
It looks good.
It looks healthy.
Bronze is a good color on you.
I look at you and I just get…
Well…
It *has* been amazing lately, hasn't it?
At least we haven't lost that.
You're so…still.
So strong.
You just…
oh, gods, it's just *incredible*
There's just this…focus.
This resolution.
Such confidence.
You used to get upset if I…
If I tried to…
you know,
push you around.
But you've been so good about just, letting me…
Take the bull by the horns.
As it were.
As they say.

(She awkwardly gets the statue down and leaned up against the chair.)

My girlfriends tell me these…
These absolute horror stories.
Their husbands get self-conscious
When their wives get on top
When they show…
uh, dominance.

And I'm just glad I married a man who's so secure in himself that he can just lie there and let me...
Take him to new worlds.

> *(She straddles the statue.)*

> (**ACASTUS** *comes on.*)

> *(There's a moment as they both look at each other, awkwardly.)*

ACASTUS/LAODAMIA. What are you doing?

> *(Beat.)*

> (**LAODAMIA** *doesn't say anything, and* **ACASTUS**, *flustered, goes to the statue and starts to lift it up.)*

ACASTUS. I'm going out
With
Him.
Protesilaos and I had
Plans
Together.

LAODAMIA. *(frantic)* Oh, that's wonderful!
It makes me so happy to see what close friends you've become.
Do you remember when we first began seeing each other, Protie?
Do you remember how Daddy acted around you?
Daddy HATED you, Protie!

ACASTUS. I never hated him.
You.
I never hated you.

LAODAMIA. Well.
You didn't exactly approve.

ACASTUS. He's too old for you.
Was too old for you.
Not *was*, that's not what I mean.
I mean, he's *still* too old for you

but I don't care anymore.
I mean, it doesn't matter as much to me.
of course I care.
But we're friends now though!
Aren't we, uh, Protie?

LAODAMIA. It makes me happy.

ACASTUS. All right.
I'll be back soon.
Don't you worry about that.

LAODAMIA. I love you both so much.
…
It's polite to say the same in return, honey.
…
Don't say you know.
Say you love me.
Tell me you love me too.
Please.
Please just.
Just tell me you love me too.
Don't go without telling me.
please.
please.

ACASTUS. I heard him.
I just heard him.

LAODAMIA. You did?

ACASTUS. He whispered it.

LAODAMIA. Oh.

ACASTUS. I don't think he's feeling well today.
That's why we're going out.
For some air.

LAODAMIA. Let me grab my coat!
I'll come too.

ACASTUS. No!!
I mean,

no.
I mean we need to have a talk.
And…

LAODAMIA. I can't come?

ACASTUS. It's.
It's man talk.
Man to man.
You understand.

LAODAMIA. Come back soon.

> (**ACASTUS** *starts dragging* **PROTESILAOS** *across the stage again.*)

Honey, why are you moving so funny?
Did you throw out your back again?
You really should be more careful, you –

ACASTUS. *He's a statue!!!!*
He's not real!
He. Is. A. Statue!!!

LAODAMIA. What?
Ha ha.
Don't say that.
Please.
Please don't say that.
Please!

ACASTUS. I'm going to destroy it.
It's not right.
It's cruel.

LAODAMIA. No!
Please.

ACASTUS. Daughter.
I have to.
I have to,
Your husband is dead.
He is dead
and he is never coming back.

LAODAMIA. Stop.
   Please.
   please.
   …
   My marriage.
   let it last a little while longer.
   Just let me have one last night with him.
   Please.

ACASTUS. You know I can't.

LAODAMIA. No!!
   no no no.

   (She goes to the statue and embraces it and nearly topples it over.)

   (ACASTUS catches it, not without pain.)

   (He lowers it down awkwardly then falls to the stage himself, in agony.)

   (He sees his daughter weeping.)

   (He embraces her on the ground.)

LAODAMIA. Father?

ACASTUS. Yes.

LAODAMIA. Can you…
   Can you tell me about mother.
   Please.
   Do you –
   Do you still miss her?

ACASTUS. Every waking moment of life.

LAODAMIA. Oh.
   …
   It's like this little hole has opened up in me
   And every time I think it's beginning to close
   a gust of air
   or a song
   or a memory of a laugh

blows it wide open again.
Does that go away?
ACASTUS. No.
But it does get easier.
LAODAMIA. When?

(Slow fade to black.)

End of Play

Time Difference

Lin Tu

TIME DIFFERENCE was first produced by Theater Masters (Julia Hansen, Artistic Director; Naomi McDougall Jones, Associate Artistic Director/Managing Director) in New York City on April 28, 2015. The performance was directed by Taylor Haven Holt. The cast was as follows:

YUAN .... Peregrine Heard
FAN .... Hugh Hyungjin Cha
ENSEMBLE. .... Jelani Alladin, Andrea Gallo, Benjamin Harris,
Heli Sirviö, Anna Weng

CHARACTERS

DARA
YUAN
SOME GUY
DENG
FAN
NARRATOR
A
B
C
D
E
F
G
AA
BB
CC
OLDER WOMAN
BRIDE
GRANDMA
BOSS ZHANG
MOTHER
ANNOYING GIRL
LOUDSPEAKER
TOM

AUTHOR'S NOTES

All the actors are on stage the entire time, acting out different characters or the background, which (I hope) could much shorten the time of lights off breaks and keep the play running fast and fluidly with no gaps.

(Loud enthusiastic people talking, noise explodes into the darkness that envelopes the whole stage, together with the background music of psychedelic rock.)

(Unidentifiable conversations. People dancing, talking, drinking, laughing.)

(Lights slowly on stage. The party shows itself. Americans, Europeans, African Americans, Asians...a group of international students that you can tell the difference merely from the appearances are immersing themselves in the delightful mood. It says "House-warming" on the banner behind.)

*(**YUAN**, an average Chinese girl in her twenties, with a drink in her hand, stands in the front. **DARA**, a middle eastern girl is talking with her. They have to shout to be heard.)*

DARA. Forgive me, what's your name again?

YUAN. Yuan.

DARA. From Beijing, right?

YUAN. Yeah!

DARA. What's your program?

YUAN. Screenwriting!

DARA. Wow, that's so cool! I can't believe I'm talking to an artist! You need to give me your signature, right now. So when I watch TV with my friends of you winning the Oscar for Best Screenplay, I could be like, "Yeah, that's the girl I once had a drink with, and a meaningful conversation!"

*(**YUAN** takes off the cap of one pen.)*

YUAN. Where shall I sign? On your shirt? Arm? Bra?

(DARA *laughs.* **SOME GUY** *bumps into her.*)

SOME GUY. Come, dance with me!

> (**YUAN** *and* **DARA** *join dancing. They dance in no particular style. Cha-cha, rabbit dance, tap dance, swing dance, folk dance...all mixed up.*)

> (*In front of the crowd, lights illuminate two Chinese young men, both in their twenties,* **FAN** *and* **DENG**. *As the conversation goes on, the party noise slowly fades away.*)

DENG. So what's her program again?

FAN. Screenwriting.

> (**DENG** *opens a bottle of beer.*)

DENG. What's she going to do with that?

> (**FAN** *opens a bottle of beer.*)

FAN. If she does well, it's money-making.

DENG. Then let's hope she won't drag my best buddy down, begging for a living on the streets.

> (*They both drink up the beer, as if a drinking contest.*)

(*placing the empty beer bottles to make a pyramid*) You know if you miss her, you could just call her.

FAN. Since when did you become all touchy-feely?

DENG. (*hitting the bottle pyramid with a baseball*) Since I'm getting married this October.

FAN. I know how tough it can be.

DENG. No you don't.

> (**FAN** *goes to pick up the baseball.*)

FAN. And it's midnight for her now.

> (*Loud party noise explodes. Flashy lights illuminate the crowd.* **FAN**, *standing in the center of downstage, turns around watching them in a frozen position.*)

(At the time, two giant digital clocks are projected onto the background. One says 12:06 a.m., Chicago Time. One says 13:06 p.m., Beijing Time.)

*(Sudden stop of the noise. Lights off. A very machine-like human voice off-stage narrates. That goes for all the **NARRATOR** parts.)*

NARRATOR. *(offstage)* 8:15 a.m., Chicago Time. 21:15 p.m., Beijing Time.

(Lights on.)

(The clocks are adjusted according to the narration, also in the following similar situations.)

(A line of people, with looks indicating different nationalities, are standing center stage. They speak one after another in a quite fast speed.)

A. Hi, I'm Brandon, from London, I like walking.

B. Hi, I'm Anna, from South Africa, I like cooking.

C. Hi, I'm Bruce, from Peru, I like drinking.

D. Olivia, Australia, jogging.

E. Yannick, Holland, hiking.

F. Camille, Monaco, painting.

G. And I like how all of you people like all of these things!

*(**YUAN** takes the hand of **G** and leads her/him and the line of people to down stage and sit down, while delivering the lines below.)*

*(**FAN** is sweeping the floors in center stage, and is revealed as the people sit down.)*

YUAN. So you get to meet all these people, all these people that were born and grew up in incredibly different countries, environments, traditions, with individual stories and childhood dreams. This Indonesian guy smokes sweet clove cigarettes that crack like fireworks when you take a drag. That Cuban girl used to be a small-town cop and has six fingers on her left hand.

And this Turkish guy says that there's this type of gathering in Turkey, where he and his friends listen to sad songs, get mopey sharing their difficulties and concerns. Can you imagine that with us?

> *(The people downstage spread into a circle, watching **FAN** and the three people surrounding him performing the next section. Some of them may stand up and act as the three people. The three talk over-dramatically, referring to **FAN** to the extent of torturing him a little bit.)*

AA. You're more successful with a beach house and a Bentley!

BB. No, you're more successful with the latest round of financing!

CC. No, you're more successful with your annual bonus of twenty thousand dollars!

AA. Your son graduated Harvard top of the class!

BB. Your dog won the state's beauty pageant five years in a row!

CC. And your TV star wife is someone everyone wants to bang!

> *(**FAN** makes a gesture as a gymnast landing and the circle applauds, while **YUAN** moves out of the circle and sits down stage, facing the audience.)*

YUAN. And sometimes, I just enjoy sitting on the sidewalk downtown, watching people passing by. Shopping bags full of high-end clothing, young lovers in their honeymoon phase who should really go get a room, tourists with baseball hats and Nikon cameras, ragged homeless people, and toddlers running loose…

> *(An **OLDER WOMAN** walks towards **YUAN** from behind, stops and yells at her.)*

OLDER WOMAN. What the fuck are you looking at? Get your ass back to China!

> *(**YUAN** chuckles.)*

YUAN. Well, there has to be exceptions.
FAN. What did you say? / Hello?
YUAN. I said I once had / an old woman yelling…
FAN. Oh I get it. It's delayed. Are / you doing well lately?
YUAN. How are you doing?
FAN. I'm / doing fine.
YUAN. Everything's fine.

> *(They smile.)*

Why are you not sleeping at midnight?
FAN. Because you're up at ten in the morning.

> *(Lights off.)*

NARRATOR. *(offstage)* *22:18 p.m., Chicago Time. 11:18 a.m., Beijing Time.*

> *(Lights on.)*

> *(With the fast version of the Wedding March music, People onstage start to act like they are joining a wedding ceremony as different characters. Someone decorating the place. Someone greeting someone. Someone conducting the band. Someone leading the way for the guests, etc…)*

> *(Unidentifiable loud conversations.)*

> *(**DENG** and his **BRIDE** marching forward, receiving blessings from surrounding people excitedly. They act in an over-exaggerated fashion.)*

BRIDE. *(to different people with a too-sweet voice)* Thank you. Oh thank you.

> *(Someone urges the **BRIDE** so she throws the bouquet to the back. The crowd spreads apart, showing **FAN** with the bouquet in his hands.)*

> *(The people suddenly surround **FAN**. Among them, **GRANDMA**, **BOSS ZHANG** and **MOTHER** talk, while others agree with stuff like "Why not," "Yeah," and nod along.)*

GRANDMA. *(with a trembling voice)* When are you getting married?

BOSS ZHANG. *(well-rounded man)* Just settle down.

GRANDMA. What do you mean you don't know?

MOTHER. Every grown-up man knows when he will get married.

BOSS ZHANG. Marriage is the medication that leads to inner peace.

GRANDMA. Look at all your cousins and friends.

MOTHER, GRANDMA & BOSS ZHANG. What are you waiting for?

>   *(**DENG** suddenly speaks.)*

DENG. Dude, don't get married.

BRIDE. *(shows her muscle, a sudden change to coarse manly voice)* Say what now?

>   *(The people dash up to stop the **BRIDE** (with words or actions) from going for **DENG**. She looks like she's going to beat him up, while **DENG** hides around. The stage becomes messy with loud noises and actions. Just when **BRIDE** ("There you are") is about to pound on **DENG**, someone shouts out.)*

SOMEONE. No!!

>   *(Everyone freezes and **YUAN** walks around these people, examining them while delivering the lines.)*

YUAN. But what used to occupy and possess my whole brain doesn't seem to bear any importance any more. It is no longer about the rules to follow and the steps to take. Shouldn't we all be free? Free from other people's supervision, the keen eyes in the name of caring, and the loving conventions that lecture you how to live?

>   *(The crowd unfreezes and starts walking about, and people keep bumping into **FAN** as he delivers his lines. He becomes more and more infuriated as he speaks on.)*

Why are you not working at twelve at noon?

FAN. Because mundaneness is really the truth of life. Because the other end of the world for you seems to be a wonderland of passion and dreams. Because passion and dreams will be washed away and eventually it's always the mundaneness of life that dominates. And because you are calling me, from the other end of the world!

(Lights off.)

NARRATOR. *(offstage)* Evening, Chicago Time. Morning, Beijing Time.

*(Softer lights on the background, spotlight on **BOSS ZHANG** and **FAN**.)*

*(**BOSS ZHANG** drags **FAN** out of the crowd [having a meeting] and taps on him hard.)*

BOSS ZHANG. You cannot talk to your client with such a temper again. But well done.

(They freeze.)

LOUDSPEAKER. *(dramatic voice)* The winner is… Cinnamon Raisin Bagel! Anyone with a winning ticket can trade your card for a full combo at any concession stand.

*(Another spotlight on a girl and **YUAN**.)*

*(**ANNOYING GIRL**, twenties, Chinese, and **YUAN** step out of the crowd look around.)*

ANNOYING GIRL. What's going on here?

LOUDSPEAKER. Do you have a lucky winner?

ANNOYING GIRL. You know how you sometimes feel the Americans are dumb, like they have to use calculators for tips, can't do mental math at all? Yet sometimes, for a game like this, even before I get it, the Americans are taking out their tickets, trying to win anything they can for free.

YUAN. Can we not use "the Americans," babe?

ANNOYING GIRL. It's one of our rare privileges to mock them in Chinese while "the Americans" around have no fucking clue what we're talking about. So babe, why not?

> *(The spotlight on **ANNOYING GIRL** and **YUAN** move to **1234** popping out of the crowd and surround **YUAN**. The following section should resemble a musical with simple choreography.)*

1. Do you know why there's always a cookie store –
2. – close to the college campus?
3. Do you know why there's always this gothic girl –
4. – hiding in the toilet stall?
1. Do you know that unique smell –
3. Do you know that non-stop laugh –
1, 2, 3 & 4. It's all because of weed. Because of weed. Because of weed.

> *(**YUAN** joins them in singing.)*

YUAN. Do you know that when you're in China, you can smoke in your office. Like in old American movies, take a drag in the bars and diners. With no Facebook and no twitter, and no weed and a lot of censors, you can smoke indoors and in winter it's the best.

> *(**BOSS** and **FAN** unfreeze.)*

BOSS ZHANG. *(to **FAN**)* Unfortunately there's no raise for you this year. But well done.

> *(They freeze.)*

> *(The spotlight on **1234** and **YUAN** moves to **TOM**, 20s, American, and **YUAN**. They step out of the crowd and act as if they're drunk. We can have the people putting down chairs for them to sit. But maybe they keep slipping off the chairs.)*

TOM. So for this survey, not just college students, but professors also voted. The No.1 "Must-do in College" is… Take a guess.

YUAN. I don't know.

TOM. A threesome.

YUAN. Really?

TOM. According to my professor, the reason that everyone votes for threesome is because there's such a small chance for you to actually have one. If you're a girl, you'd like there to be two men. If you're a guy, you'd like there to be two girls. It's impossible to satisfy the needs from both sides, that's when it becomes the golden apple.

YUAN. Interesting.

TOM. You will find out that people here talk about dirty stuff much more than people in China.

YUAN. I've realized already.

(A beat.)

TOM. You know, I kind of like you.

(A beat.)

*(***YUAN** *dives in for a wild kiss with* **TOM***. They freeze.)*

(Lights up for **FAN***.)*

FAN. There has always been this urban legend of a Chinese man studying in the States. You can't tell anything from his appearance: average, normal. But when his body was found in his house, the police found stacks of toilet paper rolls and drawers of ballpoint pens. It turned out that he replaced the full toilet paper roll with his empty one every morning when he went to the institute's bathroom, and he took a the ballpoint pen from the front desk every afternoon when he got off work.

*(***YUAN** *suddenly pushes* **TOM** *away.)*

YUAN. I'm sorry!

TOM. I'm not!

YUAN. I'm talking to myself.

FAN. Confucius brought up the idea of "Caution Action Alone." A sarcastic note on how people can really indulge themselves in off-limit craziness when there are no eyes on their backs.

(A beat.)

FAN. *(cont.)* It's 7 p.m. for you now, why are you not having dinner?

YUAN. Because you don't realize how ridiculous I feel gesturing while talking to a machine. Because your worries are powerless and unreal and I have to act like I'm moved. Because you've become less real than the signal of the cell, than the self-invited kiss. And because dinner is not important, nor is breakfast or lunch.

(Lights off.)

NARRATOR. *(offstage)* *2:15 a.m., Chicago Time. 15:15 p.m., Beijing Time.*

(Lights on.)

(YUAN is lying downstage. She slowly gets up at some point during the following conversation. FAN is standing in the middle of the crowd stage left.)

YUAN. Hello?

FAN. Hello? Can you hear me?

YUAN. No… The signal is bad.

FAN. What about now? Can you hear me? Hello?

YUAN. I can hear you now.

FAN. Anything wrong? You sound…

YUAN. All the Hong Kong protesters, Occupy Central. They can't block everything, right?

(The crowd picks up yellow umbrellas upstage and opens them and starts walking aimlessly on stage, as the conversation goes on. No particular route. Sometimes one of them stops in the middle of the stage. Sometimes a group of them fiercely run toward different directions. They bump into each other, fall on the ground, and suddenly go back to the normal pace.)

FAN. Of course they can't. There's Weibo and its millions of users. It's impossible to censor everything. And

I've climbed over the Great Firewall and read some articles…

YUAN. But it's everywhere here. You read the news, watch the clips, they're on every front page of every major magazine. You see a tear gas shell hissing through the crowds of students and the yellow umbrellas are the only weapons for them to defend themselves. Angry voices flash across the sky shadowed with confusing enthusiasm and paranoid persistence. And there's people kneeling down, beseeching the protestors to never back off until democracy and universal suffrage is regained. And then there's people kneeling down beseeching them to go home. It was all…horrifying… chaos.

(A beat. The crowd freezes.)

FAN. It's mainly just silence here in Beijing.

YUAN. Silence that we are so used to.

(A beat.)

But when your Facebook page is filled with rigorously conflicting opinions, firmly demonstrating each side, or when many of your newly-met friends from all over the world march onto the streets, holding yellow umbrellas to back up the demonstrations…

FAN. You feel like you should say something?

(A beat.)

I can still remember the stories that your dad told us about the Tiananmen Square movement.

YUAN. Yeah?

FAN. That he rode the bike alone to Tiananmen Square four o'clock the next morning. Got held up by the guard from entering. That he was standing there with a forty-year-old woman, he was then just in his twenties, and together they stared. Thick smoke scattered around army coats that were covered with yellow and black stains, and not far away on the ground was a puddle of blood. He dodged away from the guard, kicked the shell case on the ground and then scrupulously picked it up. He went back to his friend and with indignant tears in his eyes said…

YUAN. …that China is done.

>   *(A beat.)*

And I was born that year.

FAN. We were born that year.

YUAN. Then how come we grew up to be like this? To be much more concerned about losing friends than reaching a consensus through debate. To be so disconcertingly and irretrievably calm and numb towards any ambitions that promise a better world.

FAN. …It's just something we pick up along the road.

>   *(A beat.)*

They just canceled the talk a minute ago.

YUAN. Maybe I should say something.

FAN. You'd better not.

YUAN. Maybe they can understand.

FAN. But you'd better not.

>   *(The crowd gradually puts down the umbrellas and leads* **FAN** *to* **YUAN**, *and* **YUAN** *to* **FAN**.*)*

YUAN. It's 3 p.m. for you now,

FAN. It's 1 a.m. for you,

YUAN. Why are you not dozing off from paper work?

FAN. Why are you not feeling depressed in the darkness?

YUAN. Why are you not complaining about the air pollution and the sunlight trying hard to pierce through the fog?

FAN. Why are you not dreaming of chase scenes and falling off the cliff, all the bad dreams you used to talk to me about?

YUAN. Why are you not pointing out that we are walking down different roads, slowly drifting apart?

FAN. Why are you not realizing that we have passed the point of no return, or have we?

NARRATOR. *(offstage) Towards infinity, Chicago Time. Towards infinity, Beijing Time.*

YUAN. Why are you not afraid?

FAN. Why are you saying that I'm not afraid?

>   *(A beat.)*

YUAN. Should we hang up?

FAN. It's a clear morning in Beijing. Have a nice dream.

End of Play

www.ingramcontent.com/pod-product-compliance
Lightning Source LLC
Chambersburg PA
CBHW071407290426
44108CB00014B/1723